THIS LAND CALLED AMERICA: **NEW JERSEY**

CREATIVE EDUCATION

Published by Creative Education
P.O. Box 227, Mankato, Minnesota 56002
Creative Education is an imprint of The Creative Company
www.thecreativecompany.us

Design by Blue Design (www.bluedes.com)
Art direction by Rita Marshall
Book production by The Design Lab
Printed in the United States of America

Photographs by Alamy (Content Mine International, Phil Degginger, idp
eastern USA collection, Andre Jenny, Mary Evans Picture Library, North Wind
Picture Archives, Photo Network, Robert Quinlan, Rana Royalty Free, John
Van Decker), Corbis (Alan Schein Photography, Bettmann, Bob Krist, Joe
McDonald, Underwood & Underwood, Kennan Ward , David Zimmerman),
Getty Images (William Thomas Cain, Stephen Chernin, Museum of the City
of New York/Bryon Collection, Time & Life Pictures, Michael S. Yamashita),
iStockphoto (David Evans)

Library of Congress Cataloging-in-Publication Data
Wimmer, Teresa, 1975–
New Jersey / by Teresa Wimmer.
p. cm. — (This land called America)
Includes bibliographical references and index.
ISBN 978-1-58341-783-6
1. New Jersey—Juvenile literature. I. Title. II. Series.
F134.3.W56 2009
974.9—dc22   2008009512

First Edition
9 8 7 6 5 4 3 2 1

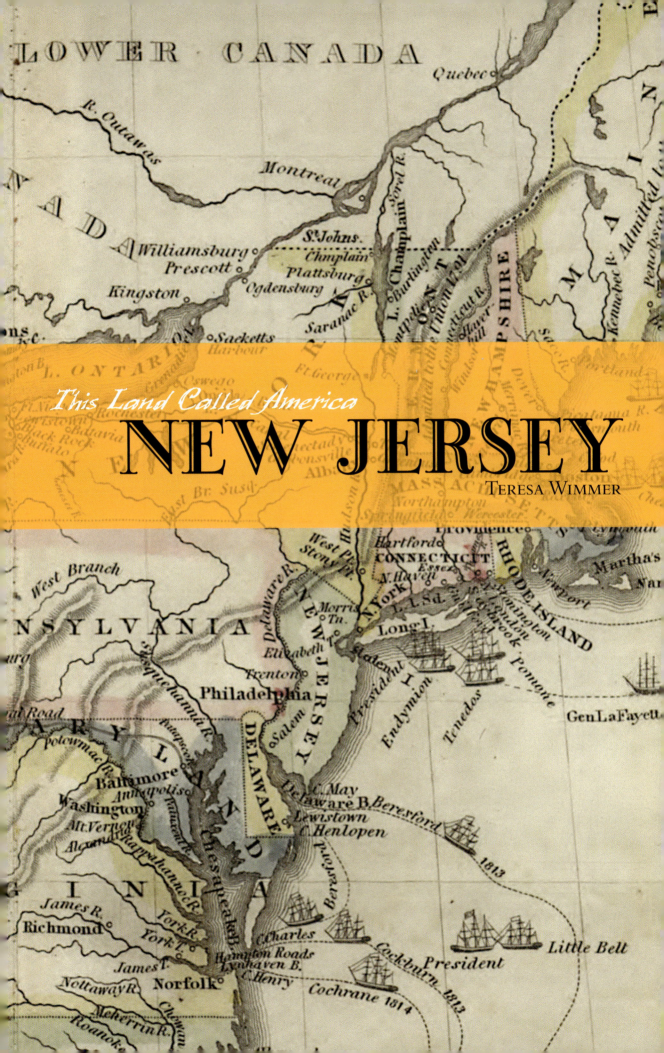

This Land Called America

NEW JERSEY

Teresa Wimmer

New Jersey

TERESA WIMMER

On a warm summer day, hundreds of families play in the hot beach sand. Many people lie on blankets to soak up the sun's rays. Children run into the Atlantic Ocean and splash one another. Farther inland, couples stroll along the boardwalk. The ocean breeze tickles their faces. When they are hungry, they stop for cotton candy at a beachside stand. Far out over the ocean, the sun is just beginning to set. The families gather their children and head for a seafood restaurant. As the day ends, they look forward to tomorrow and another day of fun on the Jersey Shore.

YEAR
1524 Italian explorer Giovanni da Verrazano becomes the first European to sail along New Jersey's coast.
EVENT

Exploring a New Land

HUNDREDS OF YEARS AGO, AMERICAN INDIAN TRIBES SUCH AS THE LENAPE (ALSO KNOWN AS THE DELAWARE) LIVED IN THE LAND NOW KNOWN AS NEW JERSEY. THEY HUNTED DEER, ELK, AND BEARS IN THE WOODLANDS, CAUGHT FISH IN THE RIVERS, GATHERED SHELLFISH FROM THE ATLANTIC OCEAN, AND PLANTED CROPS. THEY ENTERTAINED EACH OTHER WITH MUSIC, DANCES, AND STORIES.

In 1524, an Italian named Giovanni da Verrazano became the first European to see New Jersey, but he did not stay. Nearly 100 years later, in 1609, English explorer Henry Hudson sailed into New Jersey's Newark Bay. Hudson worked for the Dutch East India Trading Company, and his explorations paved the way for more Dutch settlers to come to the region. The Dutch claimed a huge area of land, which they named New Netherland.

At first, Dutch settlers got along well with the American Indians. The settlers traded knives, iron pots, clothing, and metals to the Lenape for furs. The Lenape taught the Dutch how to grow corn, beans, and squash.

In the mid-1600s, English settlers from New England and Virginia moved to New Netherland because they had heard that the land was excellent for farming. In 1664, four English

When explorer Henry Hudson (above) landed on the shores of New Jersey, he found American Indians living and hunting in the forests (opposite).

YEAR

1609   Englishman Henry Hudson explores the Sandy Hook and Newark Bay areas.

EVENT

- 7 -

An 1851 painting
by Emanuel Leutze
dramatizes George
Washington's crossing
of the Delaware River
in 1776.

An 1851 painting by Emanuel Leutze dramatizes George Washington's crossing of the Delaware River in 1776.

warships landed in New Netherland and took control from the Dutch. They split New Netherland into two lands. The southern half was given the name New Jersey.

Throughout the 1700s, New Jersey grew rapidly. More English, Dutch, Swedish, and German immigrants came to live there. Factories that made iron, glass, and paper sprang up along the colony's rivers. More wagon roads crisscrossed New Jersey than any other colony. However, not everyone benefited from New Jersey's advancements. Many Lenape died from diseases that the white settlers had brought with them, such as smallpox and tuberculosis. The Lenape who survived sold their land to white settlers in the mid-1750s and moved west.

By the late 1700s, the American colonies wanted to be independent of England. They wanted to make their own laws and govern themselves. New Jersey played an important role in the Revolutionary War, which was fought from 1775 to 1783. One stormy winter night in 1776, General George Washington and his army crossed the icy Delaware River. They landed at the town of Trenton. There, they surprised the English forces and defeated them. The Battle of Trenton helped lead to the colonies' eventual victory in the war. On December 18, 1787, New Jersey became the third state to join the newly formed United States.

Washington crosses the Delaware

YEAR
1660   Dutch settlers establish the first permanent European settlement at Bergen, which later becomes Jersey City.
EVENT

Throughout the 1800s, New Jersey continued to grow. Because it was located between the important cities of New York City to the north and Philadelphia, Pennsylvania, to the south, it needed a good transportation system. Companies in New Jersey built wagon toll roads, railroad tracks, and canals. Every day, wagons, trains, and ships carried farm produce, textiles, lumber, iron, and glass from New Jersey to sell in other states.

During the late 1800s, immigrants from European countries such as Russia, Italy, Ireland, and Poland came to New Jersey. They found work in the state's growing textile, iron, leather, and glassmaking factories. Sometimes people worked long hours for low pay, but there were always jobs available. By the beginning of the 1900s, New Jersey had become an industrial powerhouse.

Sewing machine factories such as Singer's in Elizabethport (above) produced the machines that enabled workers elsewhere to make clothing (opposite).

YEAR
1676 The New Jersey colony is divided into East Jersey and West Jersey; it reunites in 1702.
EVENT

- *10* -

Garden of Plenty

New Jersey lies on the East Coast of the U.S. in an area called the Mid-Atlantic. It is bordered on the north by New York and the Hudson River. The Delaware River and Pennsylvania lie to the west, and Delaware Bay and Delaware lie to the south. The Atlantic Ocean forms the state's eastern border.

New Jersey's land can be divided into four major regions: the Appalachian Ridge of the north, the New England Upland and Piedmont of the middle, and the Atlantic Coastal Plain of the south. The Appalachian Ridge region contains part of the Appalachian Mountain chain, including the Kittatinny Mountains. High Point is the tallest peak in the Kittatinnies, and at 1,803 feet (550 m), it is also New Jersey's highest point. Deer, black bears, and foxes roam the mountain forests. Resources such as sand, gravel, and crushed stone are mined from the mountains for use in construction.

East of the Appalachian Ridge, sparkling lakes are plentiful in the New England Upland. The lakes were created by big sheets of ice called glaciers that melted thousands of years ago. The Upland's Lake Hopatcong spans four square miles (10 sq km), which makes it New Jersey's largest lake. Peach and apple orchards also color the landscape of the Upland.

American black bears (above) are protected in many areas of the tree-covered Appalachian Mountains (opposite).

YEAR

1721

EVENT

Scottish immigrant William Trent founds Trent's Town, which later becomes the capital city of Trenton.

- 13 -

Raritan River

YEAR

1787

New Jersey becomes the third state in America on December 18.

EVENT

Farther inland from the Jersey Shore, the Pine Barrens cover more than one million acres (404,685 ha). Thousands of pine trees and hundreds of gravel roads weave through the Barrens. Not many people live there, but the sandy soil is good for growing blueberries and cranberries. Tall grasses and orchids also grow wild in the Pine Barrens.

The rest of New Jersey is also ideal for growing many different crops and flowers. That is why New Jersey is nicknamed "The Garden State." Although not many people farm, the state is a leading producer of tomatoes, sweet corn, spinach, and bell peppers. New Jersey's dairy farms also provide the country with a lot of milk.

People and animals in New Jersey contend with every type of weather. Summers are warm and humid, but cooling ocean breezes often blow in from the shore. The ocean breezes also bring the state a lot of rain each year. Winters are cool and damp. In the winter, northern New Jersey is a skier's paradise. The region averages about 50 inches (127 cm) of snow annually. However, the southern part of the state gets only about 13 inches (33 cm) of snow a year.

Cranberry harvesters must get the berries to the surface before they can collect the fruit.

YEAR

1811   The world's first steam ferryboat, the *Julianna*, begins running between Hoboken and New York City.

EVENT

- 17 -

On the Move

Today, more than 90 percent of New Jersey's residents live in cities. That is the largest percentage of city-dwellers of any state in the country. New Jersey is also the most crowded state. About 1,000 people cram into each square mile (2.6 sq km) of the state. The rest of the U.S. averages only about 85 people per square mile (2.6 sq km).

Many different people have chosen to make New Jersey their home. Today, about 65 percent of New Jersey's residents are white. African Americans and people of Hispanic heritage each make up about 15 percent of the population. A small but growing percentage of Asian Americans also live in New Jersey. Immigrants from countries such as Italy, Russia, Poland, Germany, and India find jobs in the state's factories, paper production plants, and technology industries.

Almost from the beginning, New Jersey has been situated between the major cities of New York and Philadelphia. Every day, many New Jerseyites drive across the state line to jobs in

Busy highways (above) and river ferries take people from residential New Jersey to the skyscrapers of New York City (opposite).

YEAR
1858   The first complete dinosaur skeleton in North America is discovered on farmland near Haddonfield.
EVENT

- *19* -

The Holland Tunnel, completed in 1927, was named after its engineer, Clifford Holland.

these two cities. They usually take the New Jersey Turnpike, which is the busiest road between Philadelphia and New York City. Other people drive to work through the Holland Tunnel, which runs under the Hudson River from Jersey City to New York City.

Not everyone leaves New Jersey to work, though. People in New Jersey work in factories that make electrical equipment, metal products, scientific instruments, and computers. Others make chemical and medical products such as soap, paint, and medicines. Along the Jersey Shore, fishermen gather clams, oysters, lobsters, tuna, and scallops from the Atlantic Ocean. Less than one percent of New Jersey's people

Fishing boats that patrol the waters of the Atlantic Ocean near Cape May carry large nets and ropes.

YEAR

1891

EVENT

Thomas Edison invents the world's first movie camera at his lab in West Orange.

- *20* -

farm. But the cattle, hogs, vegetables, fruits, and other plants produced on the state's farms bring in profits of about $750 million each year.

Food processing is one of New Jersey's most important industries. Many products, such as Welch's grape juice and Campbell's soup, were invented in New Jersey. Bakery goods, soft drinks, coffee, and sugar are also made in the state's processing plants.

New Jersey's people have never lost the pioneering spirit of the state's founders. Thomas Alva Edison, one of the country's most important inventors, performed most of his work in labs in West Orange and Menlo Park, New Jersey. In the late 1800s and early 1900s, Edison perfected the electric light bulb and invented phonographs and movie cameras. The city of Fort Lee became home to America's first movie studios.

Thomas Edison used his famous lab at Menlo Park from 1876 until he moved to West Orange in 1886.

Beef cattle farms throughout the state typically feed their animals a mixture of grasses and hay.

YEAR

1913   New Jersey governor Woodrow Wilson begins his first term as the 28th president of the U.S.

EVENT

New Jersey's industrial towns gave rise to many famous entertainers. Rock musician Bruce Springsteen was born in Freehold in 1949. He got his start by playing in nightclubs along the Asbury Park boardwalk. Singer and actor Frank Sinatra was born in Hoboken in 1915. Nicknamed "Old Blue Eyes," he became one of the most famous singers in the world in the 1940s. In 1954, Sinatra won an Academy Award for his performance in the movie *From Here to Eternity*.

Many writers also got their start in New Jersey. Poet

YEAR
1927
EVENT

The Holland Tunnel is completed, creating a roadway between Jersey City and New York City.

Out of the Shadows

FROM ANCIENT RELICS TO MODERN AMUSEMENTS, SIGHTSEEING IN NEW JERSEY IS A ONE-OF-A-KIND EXPERIENCE. THE NORTHWESTERN TOWNS OF FRANKLIN AND OGDENSBURG ARE HOME TO THE MOST FAMOUS ZINC MINES IN THE WORLD. MILLIONS OF YEARS AGO, MORE THAN 300 MINERALS WERE FORMED IN THE AREA'S HILLS FROM ZINC BURIED DEEP WITHIN THE EARTH. MANY OF

these minerals glow bright yellow, pink, green, and purple when put under light. Today, people can visit the Franklin Mineral Museum and search for their own buried minerals.

An important natural discovery from New Jersey's ancient past took place near Haddonfield. In 1858, geologist William Foulke discovered *Hadrosaurus foulkii*, the first complete dinosaur skeleton found in the U.S., in a local farmer's field. Today, a bronze replica of the dinosaur watches over the city's downtown. In nearby Philadelphia, Pennsylvania, visitors can get an up-close view of the original skeleton, which is on display at the Academy of Natural Sciences' Dinosaur Hall.

Natural wonders abound in New Jersey, even in its cities. In Jersey City, visitors can enjoy more than 1,500 acres (610 ha) of parkland in the middle of a bustling urban landscape. Liberty State Park provides a clear view of the Statue of Liberty, which lies just across the Hudson River near New York City. People take ferry rides to see the giant statue and walk through Ellis Island. In the late 1800s and early 1900s, many immigrants had to pass through Ellis Island before they could live in the U.S.

Ellis Island served as America's primary immigration station from 1892 until 1954.

YEAR
1952
EVENT

The New Jersey Turnpike opens and becomes the widest and busiest road in the U.S.

- 27 -

Today, the warm, sandy beaches of New Jersey's long shoreline welcome thousands of visitors. At Sandy Hook's Gateway National Recreation Area, visitors can swim, canoe, and enjoy nature walks through a forest of holly shrubs. Farther south along the Jersey Shore, the resort town of Atlantic City on Absecon Island is home to the oldest boardwalk in the country. Each year, 30 million people travel to Atlantic City. Kids can enjoy the rides and cotton candy at the city's amusement park, and adults can gamble in the many casinos.

Farther inland, people can enjoy the great outdoors on horseback. New Jersey has more horses per square mile (2.6 sq km) than any other state in the country. The Piedmont region is dotted with many horse pastures and stables. Each August, the city of East Rutherford hosts Hambletonian Day, one of the country's top harness races (a special type of horse-racing).

The boardwalk along the ocean at Atlantic City is lined with carnival rides and amusements.

YEAR

1995   The New Jersey Devils hockey team wins the Stanley Cup, claiming the state's first pro sports championship.

EVENT

QUICK FACTS

Population: 8,685,920

Largest city: Newark (pop. 280,135)

Capital: Trenton

Entered the union: December 18, 1787

Nickname: Garden State

State flower: purple violet

State bird: eastern goldfinch

Size: 8,721 sq mi (22,587 sq km)—47th-biggest in U.S.

Major industries: manufacturing, food processing, farming, fishing, tourism

New Jerseyites enjoy rooting for their favorite professional sports teams—which are often shared with their New York neighbors. The National Football League's New York Giants and New York Jets play their home games in East Rutherford's Giants Stadium, which is also known as the Meadowlands. Other professional teams share the state's name: hockey's New Jersey Devils, basketball's New Jersey Nets, and soccer's New Jersey Ironmen. Another pro soccer team, the New York Red Bulls, also plays at the Meadowlands.

Even as it has become the crossroads of the East Coast, New Jersey has managed to maintain the beauty of its sandy beaches, glistening waters, and majestic hills. Many pleasant days for horseback riding, swimming, biking, and canoeing keep visitors coming back again and again. Every day, people who venture into New Jersey's back roads are surprised by the bounties that the Garden State has to offer.

YEAR

2007 The Prudential Center opens in Newark to host hockey and soccer games, as well as concerts.

EVENT

BIBLIOGRAPHY

Fleming, Thomas. *New Jersey: A History*. New York: W. W. Norton & Company, 1977.

Foulke, Patricia, and Robert Foulke. *A Visitor's Guide to Colonial & Revolutionary Mid-Atlantic America*. Woodstock, Vt.: Countryman Press, 2007.

Kiniry, Laura. *Moon Handbooks: New Jersey*. Emeryville, Calif.: Avalon Travel, 2006.

Stansfield, Charles A. *A Geography of New Jersey: The City in the Garden*. Piscataway, N.J.: Rutgers University Press, 1998.

State of New Jersey. "Homepage." The State of New Jersey. http://www.state.nj.us.

INDEX